Getting With It:

A Kid's Guide to Forming Good Relationships and "Fitting In"

by

Kim "Tip" Frank, Ed.S., LPC
Counselor/Psychotherapist
Rock Hill School District
Family Counseling and
  Play Therapy Services
Rock Hill, SC

Susan J. Smith-Rex, Ed.D.
College of Education
Winthrop University
Rock Hill, SC

Illustrations coordinated by Ruth Ann Jackson and Jan Hanna Elliott
Cover drawing by Derek Brown

Copyright 1997

Educational Media Corporation®
P.O. Box 21311
Minneapolis, MN 55421-0311

(612) 781-0088

ISBN 0-932796-77-X

Library of Congress Catalog No. 97-60032

Printing (Last Digit)

9 8 7 6 5 4 3 2

Educational Media Corporation® reserves all rights to the materials in this book under U.S. copyright laws. In an effort to provide educational materials which are as practical and economical as possible, we grant to *individual* purchasers of this book the right to make copies of material contained therein for their personal use only. This permission is *limited* to a single person, and does not apply to entire schools or school systems. Additional copies of this book should be purchased for each teacher or counselor for use with their students. Copying this book or its parts for resale is strictly prohibited.

Production editor—
   Don L. Sorenson, Ph.D.

Graphic Design—
   Earl Sorenson

Illustrators—

Nicole Hamilton	Maggie McCaskill	Jason Elkins
Stephen Price	Jeff Stewart	James Bender
Patrick Sippel	Anne Price	Phu Nguyen
Im Chan	Keith Elliott	Allison Hope Ferguson
Eve Najim	John Wilson	Katherine Gillen
Derek Brown	Jan Hanna Elliott	Ashley Gatlin

Special thanks to B.J. Currence of York, SC; Debbie Howard of Rock Hill, SC; and Michael Kushler of Fort Mill, SC for practicing and successfully using the ideas in this book.

Note to Parents and Health Professionals:

This book is intended to aid children in the appropriate use of verbal and nonverbal communications. The term *social cognition* describes an area of difficulty with which many students struggle. Students may be oblivious to the effect their behavior is having on their peers and they may have difficulty putting themselves in someone else's shoes. This book was carefully written to be user friendly for children. We trust the vocabulary, illustrations, and limited number of words on each page will make this book inviting and helpful to children in their understanding of what is usually considered socially acceptable behavior.

The second part of this book focuses on practical ideas children can use to increase their social consciousness. We believe in children's abilities to distinguish appropriate levels of behavior. This section is interactive in nature. The student selects areas of concern and does activities which will help the child explore what needs to be done to feel comfortable, confident, and accepted. In essence, self-help projects are provided that are practical and thought-provoking.

While this book can be used independently by elementary and middle school students, we highly recommend parents, teachers, and mental health professionals read and discuss this book with children. In this way the information and suggestions are fully discussed and the children are encouraged to follow through on the strategies provided. Best wishes as you put this book to good use!

Kim "Tip" Frank, Ed.S., LPC

Susan J. Smith-Rex, Ed.D.

Getting With It

Ashley Gatlin

Table of Contents

Forward: Note to Parents and Health Professionals 3

Part I **Helping Children Understand the Importance of "Fitting In" and "Feeling Comfortable"** 7

Part II **Practical Ideas to Increase Good Social Skills, Friendships and Assertiveness Skills** 27

Terms 28

    A. Social Skills—Verbal and Nonverbal Communication 29

    B. Being a Good Friend to Yourself 45

    C. Being a Friend to Others—The Friendship Model 48

    D. Assertiveness Skills—Letting Others Know How You Feel and What You Need 55

    E. Identifying Your Support System 60

References 63

Part I

Helping Children Understand the Importance of "Fitting In" and "Feeling Comfortable"

Nicole Hamilton

It is probably true that our world puts too much importance on the three B's—Beauty, Brains, and Brawn (muscle). Actions such as kindness, good behavior, and unselfishness are often not rewarded enough in our everyday life, even though most people wish they were.

Maggie McCaskill

"Fitting in" and "feeling comfortable" around others are skills that take as much talent as doing well in music, sports, or school.

Jason Elkins

Not all people have the natural ability to figure out what to say or how to act to make others enjoy being around them. It is important to be yourself, but in order not to feel lonely you also need to "fit in."

Stephen Price

Most people think words are the most important part of communicating with others. The truth is that it is often our actions that others see as being "cool" or "strange."

Jeff Stewart

We communicate not only by talking, but also through what is called body language. Without saying a word, we can communicate or send messages to others. We send messages, for example, through the expressions on our faces, our body movements, and physical mannerisms.

A Kid's Guide to Forming Good Relationships and "Fitting In"

James Bender

If we behave in a way that people around us consider odd or inappropriate, there is a chance of being left out.

Patrick Sippel

Social cues are happening around us all the time. Social cues are the little things that people do that tell us how to act in certain situations. For example, a smile should bring a friendly response in return. Or a friend walking quickly by may be a cue that now is not a good time to talk.

A Kid's Guide to Forming Good Relationships and "Fitting In"

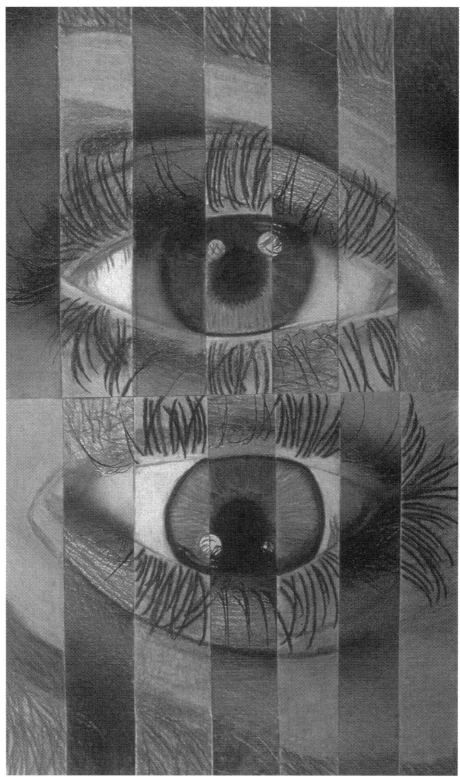

Anne Price

A person who has trouble reading these cues and sending appropriate social cues may be considered odd or different.

Phu Nguyen

When we are not accepted or liked by others, this often brings about unhappy feelings within ourselves. This is called poor self-esteem. While many people struggle to feel good about themselves, it surely helps when we feel liked by others.

A Kid's Guide to Forming Good Relationships and "Fitting In"

Im Chan

How can we gain a feeling of belonging and acceptance from those around us? Later in this book we will look at many ways people send signals or messages to others without even saying a word. If you can master the art of using good social skills (which anyone can learn), you will be successful in most situations with others.

Getting With It

Keith Elliott

On the following pages is the story of Bud. Notice the ways Bud turns people "off" by his behavior. He often makes bad choices. As you read each cartoon, list Bud's "bloopers" or mistakes beneath each cartoon. Bud's "Bloopers" are humorous and a bit exaggerated, but there are lessons in them for all of us.

On the next page is a list of social mistakes that people sometimes make. Look at this list carefully before reading the story of Bud's "Bloopers."

18 Kim "Tip" Frank, Ed.S., LPC and Susan J. Smith-Rex, Ed.D.

A Kid's Guide to Forming Good Relationships and "Fitting In"

Things to Keep in Mind When Around Others

Punctuality—	Planning ahead and being on time
Facial Expressions—	Understanding the expressions or looks on others' faces and sending appropriate expressions back
Eye Contact—	Looking at the eyes of the other person without staring
Posture—	Standing or sitting in a way that "fits" the situation
Appearance—	Wearing appropriate clothing for the situation
Voice Tone—	"How" something is said which shows how you feel
Rate of Speech—	The speed with which you talk
Voice Volume—	The loudness or softness of your voice
Personal Hygiene—	Looking clean and smelling nice
Rhythm and Pace—	Recognizing the speed of others and matching their pace
Manners—	Being polite and acting appropriately toward others
Mannerisms—	Little habits that you do over and over
Personal Space—	The distance or space that you allow between yourself and others
Touch—	Touching others only at appropriate times and in appropriate ways
Gestures—	Knowing what arm, hand, or finger motions to use and when it is appropriate
Walking—	Walking in ways to send appropriate messages or signals to others

Getting With It

1.

Bud is determined to get his first date. He has always had trouble attracting any friends—especially a girlfriend. He is, however, clueless as to why he can't seem to connect with other people. To his credit, he appears to be friendly and never mean to others. However, he has a knack for doing the wrong thing at the wrong time.

2.

Bud's quest for a date with Betty Lou got off to a bad start. After a lot of thinking, Bud decides at 6:30 a.m. on a Saturday morning that Betty Lou is the girl he has been waiting for his whole life. Bud climbs out of bed and walks over to Betty Lou's house. Before leaving, he grabs some leftover pizza to eat on the way.

Social Mistakes:

3.

Upon arriving at Betty Lou's house at 6:45 a.m., there is no sign of life. Bud begins ringing the doorbell. When no one answers, Bud begins pounding on the door as he sings a popular rap song.

Social Mistakes:

4.

The door opens and a large man stands at the door. This man, with a scowl on his face, gruffly says, "What do you want?" Not noticing Betty Lou's father was more than just a little mad, Bud stares directly at his feet, with his back hunched over and his belly hanging over his jeans.

Social Mistakes:

A Kid's Guide to Forming Good Relationships and "Fitting In"

5.

Bud says, while still eating leftover pizza and mumbling in a very low voice, "Can I talk to Betty Lou?" At this point, Betty Lou's father shouts, "Get out of here and don't ever come back again." Then he slams the door in Bud's face.

Social Mistakes:

6.

Bud wonders, "What's wrong with him?" He is not going to let this "little incident" keep him from the girl of his dreams. He goes home and plots his strategy.

Social Mistakes:

7.

Remembering the school dance is tonight and that certainly Betty Lou would be there, Bud decides that he'll spend the evening with her at the dance.

Social Mistakes:

8.

Meanwhile, Bud gets busy doing other things. He changes a flat tire and readjusts the chain on his bike, leaving his hands a greasy mess. Then he goes fishing the rest of the day. Before he knows it, it is after 7:00 p.m.

Social Mistakes:

Getting With It

9.

Suddenly Bud's thoughts turn back to Betty Lou and the dance which started at 7:00. He doesn't have time to shower and put on clean clothes if he is going to spend the entire evening with Betty Lou. Moments later he shows up at the school dance smelling of sweat, which he tried to cover up with strong cologne and deodorant.

Social Mistakes:

10.

Realizing time is fleeting, Bud rushes frantically into the school dance, nearly knocking people over while looking for Betty Lou. In a loud voice, Bud inquires about the whereabouts of Betty Lou with everyone he sees. Bud keeps interrupting people who are talking.

Social Mistakes:

11.

Bud grabs each person he can find, trying to locate his imagined date.
He also points and waves at everyone, trying to get their attention. Bud gives high-5's to several classmates.
He accidently knocks one girl over.

Social Mistakes:

12.

At long last, Bud sees Betty Lou. Not noticing that she already has a date, Bud walks right up to Betty Lou and gives her a bear hug. In shock, Betty Lou breaks away.

Social Mistakes:

A Kid's Guide to Forming Good Relationships and "Fitting In"

13.

Bud insists that she dance with him, not noticing the look of disgust on her face. Bud draws Betty Lou near him on the dance floor, and he runs his greasy hand down her cheek.

Social Mistakes:

14.

In the meanwhile, Betty Lou's date returns. Bud does not notice him and continues to dance with Betty Lou as she struggles to get away. Betty Lou keeps turning her head away from Bud when he talks because his breath smells like garlic. At this point, Mike, Betty Lou's date, physically grabs and throws Bud out the door head first.

Social Mistakes:

15.

drawings by Jan Hanna Elliott

Bud is still clueless about what went wrong. Let's look at his behaviors which turned people "off." See how many you caught in the story. We counted many inappropriate behaviors. (see page 24)

Our "Blooper" Score

Appropriate Social Skills	Bud's Social Mistakes
Punctuality—planning ahead and being on time	• Showing up at Betty Lou's too early • Losing track of time and being late for the dance
Facial expressions—understanding the expressions on other's faces and sending appropriate expressions.	• Bud missed the scowl on the father's face. He also missed the disgusted look on Betty Lou's face.
Eye Contact—looking at the eyes of the other person without staring	• Bud grabbed others and got in their faces (staring) • Bud stared at his feet when Betty Lou's father asked him a question.
Posture—positioning one's body to send appropriate messages	• Standing hunchbacked with his belly hanging over his belt.
Appearance	• Bud was dressed in dirty clothes, which were not appropriate for a dance.
Voice Tone	• Calling out for Betty Lou at the dance • Talking too low and mumbling to Betty Lou's father
Rate of Speech	• Talking too fast
Voice Volume	• Talking too loud at the dance
Personal Hygiene (cleanliness)	• Not clean—too much cologne • Bad breath (pizza breath) • Dirty clothes and hands
Rhythm and Pace—recognizing the speed of others and matching their pace	• Frantically running around looking for Betty Lou
Manners	• Interrupting others while trying to find Betty Lou • Bud never introduced himself to Betty Lou's father
Mannerisms	• Singing at an inappropriate time
Personal Space	• Getting in people's faces while trying to find Betty Lou
Touch	• Grabbing others and giving high-5's that were too hard • Hugging Betty Lou and running a hand down her cheek
Gestures—knowing arm, hand, or finger motions to use and when they are appropriate	• Wildly pointing and waving at everyone at the dance
Walking (Gait)	• Walking in a hurry—nearly knocking people over

A Kid's Guide to Forming Good Relationships and "Fitting In"

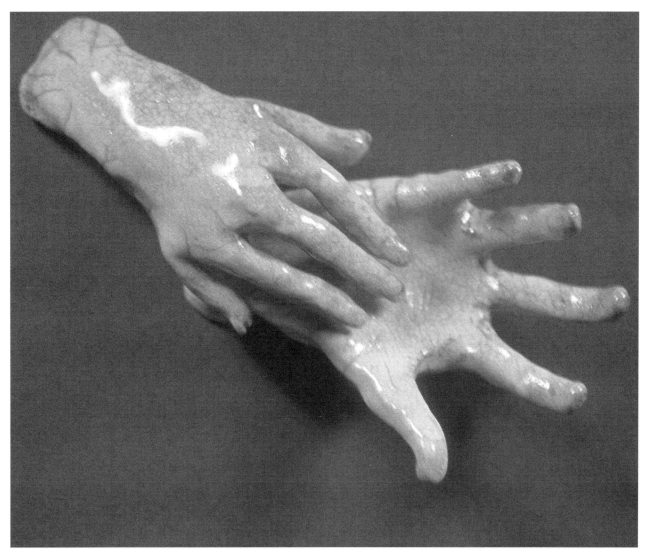

Allison Hope Ferguson

Although most people occasionally make social mistakes, making them too often will cause others to shy away. Understanding appropriate ways to act will be a big step towards "getting with it."

Educational Media Corporation®, Box 21311, Minneapolis, MN 55421-0311

Good listener

SENSITIVE

Patient *Good posture*

PUNCTUAL

Shares

Moderate

Friendly

POLITE

Clean

Flexible

Good eye contact

Part II

Practical Ideas to Increase Good Social Skills, Friendships, and Assertiveness Skills

Terms

1. **Appearance** — The way you physically present yourself in public

2. **Intensity Barometer** — An instrument that measures strength of behavior

3. **Eye Contact** — An ability to look into the eyes of someone with whom you are talking

4. **Facial Expressions** — The way a person's face looks that shows different feelings

5. **Gait** — Your style of walking

6. **Gesture** — Moving your body or limbs as a way of expressing yourself

7. **Intensity** — The strength or energy level

8. **Manners** — Good social behavior

9. **Mannerisms** — Little things people do that become habits

10. **Moderate** — A comfortable level of behavior

11. **Nonverbal Communications** — Your way of communicating through your behavior

12. **Personal Hygiene** — The way you demonstrate good health

13. **Personal Space** — The distance you usually like to maintain from another person

14. **Posture** — The position of your body

15. **Punctuality** — Being prompt and on time

16. **Rate of Speech** — The speed at which you talk

17. **Verbal Communications** — The way you communicate with words

18. **Voice Tone** — The feelings heard in a person's voice

A. Social Skills—
Verbal and Nonverbal Communications

Every day we communicate with others by sending messages and receiving messages. Most people believe this is done solely by talking and listening to others. However, most (57%) of our communication is done nonverbally (without talking). In the information which follows, consider how each nonverbal communication skill can affect you or others.

1. **Punctuality** means being prompt and on time. When you show up at the time that was requested, it tells others that you are courteous and respectful of everybody else. When you are often late or too early, people feel they can't really count on you. Consider how you are in regards to your punctuality at home, in school, and with your friends. If others get frustrated with you or tease you about being late or showing up at the wrong time, you need to think about improving this area.

    Being on time is a quality that you will need as you get older if you hope to get a job or be successful in life. If you think that others don't care about your punctuality, you are ***wrong!*** Think hard about the importance of being on time and the message you send to other people.

2. **Facial expressions** are the different signs on your face that express feelings. Without talking you can change your facial signs to communicate happiness, anger, sadness, friendship, and so forth. Pay attention to the messages people send you and the messages you send to others through various facial expressions. It is important to display clear messages rather than muddy messages if you want others to enjoy being around you. Look into a mirror and notice what happens to your eyebrows, lips, and eyes as your feelings change. Also, notice the facial expressions of friendly people. Work hard to make your facial expressions positive and clear. Other people will enjoy your presence much more.

   Keeping a pleasant look on your face is a key to building good relationships with others. Also, pay close attention to the expressions on other people's faces. Get to know what others are saying with their faces. If you miss a smile, scowl, or a disgusted look, for example, then you'll not know how to respond.

3. **Eye contact** is the ability to look into the eyes of the people around you without staring at them. When you look into the eyes of the person with whom you are communicating, it shows you feel good about yourself. Others are naturally attracted to people who feel good about themselves. When you are nervous, scared, or intimidated, you will probably find it harder to display strong eye contact. You may need to practice the skill of good eye contact in the privacy of your own home with a mirror. Talk to yourself and look into your own eyes. Practice doing the same with family members. Make it a comfortable habit so that you will be able to establish good eye contact with your peers and teachers.

   Eve Najim

4. **Posture,** or the way in which you stand or sit, communicates to others a level of self-confidence and basic interest and support. If you sit slumped over in a seat, others may interpret the behavior as rude, not caring, or immature. If you walk with your shoulders hunched over, this behavior may be interpreted as weak, scared, or shy. Evaluate your posture as you sit, stand, and walk. Make it a habit to sit up and walk tall. Present yourself in a positive way at all times. You are worth it!

5. The way you **dress and appear** to others is an important aspect of acceptance. Most people like to feel "cool" and "fashionable." It is good to display your unique features, but if you go to the extreme, you may be considered "odd" and may not "fit in." Try to find a **moderate** way of presenting yourself so that negative attention is not directed towards you.

Notice the style and dress of others around you. Certain hair styles, clothes, and jewelry may be "in." Fads constantly change, but meeting certain peer standards can be important. It shows you are part of the group. These styles of dress and appearance do not need to be expensive. Also, it should be noted *not* to *compromise* or change your values or beliefs to "fit in." You must always feel comfortable with what the group wants you to do or be. There is a balance of "being yourself" and "fitting in" that everyone must find.

Your physical appearance should not be overlooked. Exercising your body and eating right are two important disciplines. While we all have a basic shape and size, we can control a lot about our appearance. Having muscle tone and keeping weight under control add to our self-esteem. This in turn helps us to connect well with others.

6. **Voice tone, rate of speech, and volume** refers to the style, speed and loudness in which you speak. Finding a moderate level is important. Your family and peers will enjoy being around you much more if you are not yelling, mumbling, whispering, or jumbling words together.

Your voice needs *expression*. In other words, as the tone of your voice changes, this will make you sound like a more interesting person. Guard against a monotone voice. This means talking in a way that sounds always the same or boring. Another problem can be if you sound uneducated. Poor grammar or too much of an accent may cause rejection by others.

Your *rate of speech* is important also. If you talk too slowly, you will come off as slow or not very smart. If you speak too fast, you will appear hyper or too active.

The *volume* of your voice also is critical. Talking too loudly turns others off, while talking too softly makes you hard to understand.

One final caution is to watch how much you talk. When you constantly talk without listening to others, it wears others out. Don't be a "motor mouth."

Read a paragraph into a tape recorder and listen to your volume, tone, and rate of speech. It might also be fun to tape a conversation with a friend or at home to hear how you sound.

7. **Personal hygiene.** For the sake of your health as well as being accepted by others, you must take care to be neat and clean. Seemingly little things such as combing your hair, bathing regularly, using deodorant, brushing your teeth, and wearing clean clothes make all the difference in being included or left out. In our world it is very important to look right and to smell right. While this can be taken to an extreme, personal hygiene is a key to fitting in. We encourage you to take extra time to prepare yourself each day so you will look and feel clean. Even one thing such as having bad breath or being sweaty will certainly turn others off.

    Your body is wonderfully made. Take care of it.

8. **Rhythm and pace** involve your activity level. The trick here is to notice the speed at which others are going around you. According to the situation, people move faster or slower. Being out of rhythm with others will cause problems. For instance, if your family has to wait for you to slowly get ready for school day after day, frustration is soon to follow. On the other hand, at recess if you run circles around the other kids, you will wear them out.

    Each situation has a speed or rhythm about it which is set by the people involved. In some situations it is good to be "laid back." In others, you must pick up the pace. Be aware of what is going on around you and set your pace. Practice going at the speed or pace of those around you in the home, classroom, recess time, church, and so forth.

Getting With It

9. **Manners** can take you a long way in life. Bad manners, on the other hand, really turn people off. Note the bad manners listed below. Hopefully, not many of them involve you.

Types of People with Bad Manners

1. **Hogs**—People who don't know how to share and take turns.
2. **Whiners**—People that whine and complain when they don't get their way.
3. **Big Mouths**—People who can't shut up. They constantly talk, usually about themselves or other people.
4. **Gross Outs**—People who burp and pass gas among other gross things they often do. Other gross things include yawning, sneezing, and coughing without covering their mouth. They also talk with a mouth full of food. Others have an annoying habit of constantly scratching.
5. **All Hands People**—People who push, poke, and touch people when they shouldn't. They also take things from others. They are all hands and no head.
6. **Butinskys**—People who constantly interrupt others and blurt out their ideas.
7. **The Wrecking Crew**—People who wreck other people's property and who don't put things back where they belong.
8. **Rude Rowdies**—People who can't remember to say please, thank you, excuse me, and so forth.
9. **Bargers**—People who enter rooms without knocking. They also look at other people's private materials.

Good manners show others that you are thoughtful and caring. As the golden rule states, "Treat others the way you want them to treat you." How do you treat others?

10. **Mannerisms** are little habits and things we do over and over. Pretty much anything that is done too often will bring social problems. Sometimes we have habits of which we are not aware. Here is a list of some of the mannerisms that tend to cause social problems:

   sniffing

   biting fingernails

   coughing

   clearing throat

   twirling hair

   scratching

   playing with objects

   It is important to note that some people cannot control some of these behaviors due to certain medical conditions. Most people, however, can change constant behaviors and habits by becoming more aware of what they are doing and working on it. Counseling can also help. Take a few minutes to think about any behaviors you may do too often. Remember you can change yourself.

Getting With It

11. **Personal space**. We all need a certain amount of space to feel comfortable. Have you ever had someone stand too close while talking to you? Have you ever had someone you didn't know sit right next to you, even though there were many empty seats around? Chances are you felt very uncomfortable. Respecting others' personal space is crucial. Below is a drawing which gives guidelines for how close you should be in relation to others.

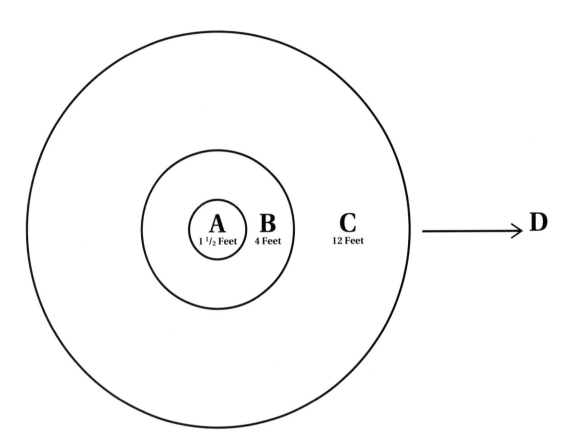

Zone A is used for family and close friends. Talk in this zone is about feelings and more personal things. (Touch to 1 1/2 feet)

Zone B is used for friends and acquaintances. Conversations are fairly quiet about everyday things (weather, sports, school, etc.). (Up to 4 feet)

Zone C is used for louder talk such as greetings and friendly conversation (chit chat). (Up to 12 feet)

Zone D: Beyond 12 feet we do not usually talk to others. Gestures and postures are used.

Pay attention to your situation and judge what distance you need to keep from others. Practice keeping safe boundaries which will help others to enjoy being with you more.

12. **Touch**. In our culture, the rules for touching others need to be carefully observed. Touching others in inappropriate ways can get you in real trouble. There are two major things to think about when you decide to touch another person. They are *location* (where you touch another) and *intensity* (how soft or hard you touch).

Location: Notice the body drawing below which in general describes acceptable versus unacceptable touching with those around you.

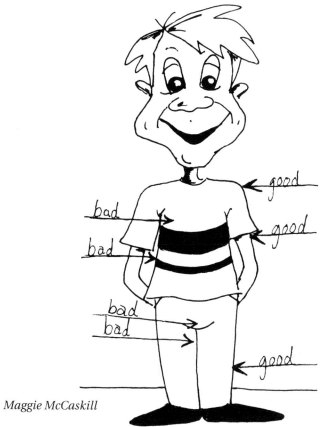

Maggie McCaskill

Note that the acceptable areas are on the outside of the bodyline (outside of the arms, outside of the legs, and the top of the shoulder). Unacceptable areas involve the inside of the bodyline (inside of the arms, the sides of the chest, the inside of the legs and thighs, the stomach, and the private parts).

Intensity: How you touch others is worth discussing. Patting someone softly when that person does something well is appropriate, while poking another is almost always disliked. Squeezing can be good or bad depending on the *intensity*. A whimpy handshake, for example, may make you look weak. A handshake that is too hard or a hug that is too strong may hurt or bother another person. You need to find the right intensity or strength when touching another.

Watch other people, especially adults, and notice how, when, and where they touch others. The rules for good touching and bad touching are learned by observing others. It is important for the most part to keep your hands and feet to yourself. There are plenty of situations where touching is appropriate. Just remember our two words—*intensity* and *location*.

13. **Gestures**. We often make motions with our bodies that send messages to others. These gestures are often used with words; however, sometimes gestures are made without using words. You need to know which gestures to use and when to use them. Look at the words below and create a gesture that communicates the message.

   1. Friendly wave
   2. Stop
   3. I don't know
   4. Calm down
   5. I mean business
   6. Come here
   7. Go away
   8. Ta Da

Children who can make clear gestures to communicate have a real advantage over other children. They are better understood. On the other hand, children who can read these gestures know how to respond correctly to the situation.

One must know which gestures to use and which ones not to use. For example, a child who comes across in a bossy way by pointing at others, much like a teacher would use to get children to behave, will be disliked. This is more of an adult gesture. On the other hand a person who learns to express feelings such as friendliness with a kind waving gesture will be well received.

Watch a TV show and pay close attention to the gestures. It is fun to turn off the volume and try to understand what is happening by watching gestures and facial expressions.

14. **Walk (Gait)**. Like postures, the way we walk tells others a lot. When you walk, feelings are often communicated. Stomping your feet shows anger, for example. A child skipping shows happiness. Sometimes, however, your feelings don't match your walking posture. For example, you may walk in a way which makes you look mean when you may actually be trying to make friends. You may need to walk in a more relaxed way to show you are friendly.

What is your gait or style of walking? Again watch how people walk and what you think they are saying with their style. Part of "fitting in" involves learning how to appropriately communicate your feelings through how you walk.

John Wilson

Role Play Situations

Below is a list of ten situations in which a student is communicating either at a very low or very high intensity level. In small groups, act out each situation and discuss how to show a **moderate** acceptable behavior level. Next, fill out your own intensity barometer on the next page.

1. While talking to a peer, look down at your feet.

2. While listening to your parent, have a disgusted look on your face.

3. During class, slump down in your seat and rest your head in your hand.

4. Enter class pretending that you've dyed your hair green, tattooed both arms, pierced your nose, and placed ten chains around your neck.

5. While walking into the cafeteria, yell out to several friends at the other end of the room.

6. Go up to your principal to ask a question. Your principal has to ask you four times to repeat yourself because you mumble and are so soft spoken.

7. A speaker circulates around the room shaking each student's hand. Your handshake is whimpy!

8. While walking down the hall, a school bully motions to you in a frightening way.

9. While talking to a student and invading that person's personal space, that student slowly backs away from you.

10. During a class lecture, the students stare at you as you tap your pencil continuously on your desk.

Your Own Personal Intensity Barometer

Put an "X" under low, medium, or high for each area.
Do you feel you have too little, too much, or just the right intensity level?

	low	medium	high
Confident posture			
Appropriate handshake, hugs, or high 5			
Appropriate use of gestures			
Good eye contact			
Friendly smile			
Good voice quality			
Appropriate laugh			
Good physical health			
Neatness			

Checklist on Nonverbal Communication: How Are You Doing?

Rate yourself on a scale of 1 to 3 by circling the appropriate number.
  1   =   needs improvement
  2   =   ok
  3   =   very good

1. Punctuality
   Are you on time? (not too early or too late)
        1   2   3
2. Facial Expressions
   Is your face friendly and appealing?
        1   2   3
   Do you notice the expression on other faces and respond appropriately to them?
        1   2   3
3. Eye Contact
   Do you look at the eyes of others while talking without staring?
        1   2   3
4. Posture
   Do you stand tall and sit up straight?
        1   2   3
5. Dress and Appearance
   Are you moderate in your dress and appearance?
        1   2   3
6. Voice Tone—Rate of Speech—and Volume
   Do you vary your tone of voice to sound interesting?
        1   2   3
   Do you speak clearly and use a moderate rate of speech?
        1   2   3
   Are you using an appropriate volume according to the situation?
        1   2   3

7. **Personal Hygiene**

    Are you regularly neat and clean?

        1   2   3

8. **Rhythm and Pace**

    Do you match the speed and pace of those around you?

        1   2   3

9. **Manners**

    Do you treat others the way you want to be treated?

        1   2   3

10. **Mannerisms**

    Do you avoid habits that annoy others?

        1   2   3

11. **Personal Space**

    Do you keep an appropriate distance from others?

        1   2   3

12. **Touch**

    Do you keep your hands and feet to yourself for the most part?

        1   2   3

    When you touch others is it done with the right location and intensity?

        1   2   3

13. **Gestures**

    Do you pick up on the gestures of others and respond appropriately?

        1   2   3

    Do you send appropriate gestures that communicate well with others?

        1   2   3

14. **Walking and Gait**

    Do you walk in a way that communicates your true feelings?

        1   2   3

Personal Prescription

Once you have had a chance to rate yourself on your barometer and checklist, select three to five behaviors that you would like to improve. List them on your personal prescription and place it in spots where you can encourage yourself to pay attention to these behaviors. It is important to monitor yourself!

(Place it on your desk, notebook, or your bathroom mirror.)

Example:

> Don't Forget To:
> 1. Be ready on time!
> 2. Smile often
> 3. Look people in the eyes
> 4. Stand and sit tall
> 5. Speak up and speak clearly

Blank:

> Don't Forget To:
> 1.
> 2.
> 3.
> 4.
> 5.

B. Being a Good Friend to Yourself

Clear Messages

One of the first relationships to consider is the relationship you have with yourself.

I'm thinking of a person who is very important and special. This person is someone you see every day. This person is also one of the most important friends you could ever have. Can you name this person?

The answer is **YOU!** Sometimes we forget to be thankful for the good things in our lives when we are concerned about fitting in and having confidence. One thing to keep in mind is that people are not perfect. Feeling down on yourself much of the time is unproductive and will hurt your self-esteem.

The best way to feel better about yourself is to change your way of thinking. Your thinking can either work for you or against you. You have basically two ways of thinking about yourself and the things that happen to you. We call them *muddy* messages and *clear* messages.

Muddy messages are thoughts that cause you to feel bad about yourself. This is when you feel upset inside and things bother you.

Clear messages are just the opposite. These thoughts make you feel good about yourself. You feel at peace inside and things don't bother you.

Here are some examples of clear versus muddy thinking.

Event	Muddy Message	Clear Message
Someone calls you a name.	"Everyone thinks I'm a jerk."	"People who call names are just trying to get others upset. I'm not going to pay attention to him."
You aren't invited to a party.	"What's the point in trying? I'll never be popular."	"I wish I would have been invited, but I'm still an okay person. Not everyone is going, so I'll plan something with other friends."

Self-Talk

What you say to yourself makes all the difference. This is called *self-talk*. To feel good about yourself, it is important to think good thoughts. Good thoughts equal good feelings. Remember we all have things we're not really good at doing. It is okay not to be good at some things. What's important is to do your best and learn to like yourself.

One of the most important self-talk words to remember is *IALAC*. It stands for I Am Lovable and Capable. *Lovable* means people can love you just because of who you are. You are special not because of what you do but who you are. *Capable* means you can. You can do many things well. Take a minute to list at least two things you do well at school and outside of school.

In School   Out of School

1. _____   1. _____

2. _____   2. _____

IALAC

On an index card, write the word IALAC. Let this be your secret code word. Take it with you to remind you that you are special and okay.

IALAC is a wonderful clear message. There are many more that you can say to yourself. Try the following experiment this week. Every time something happens to you good or bad, give yourself a clear message. Catch your muddy messages and change them to clear messages. Remember, you control what you think. No junk thoughts! Practice using clear messages such as:

"I'm okay."

"I can handle it."

"I'll just do my best."

"No one is perfect."

"It's going to work out."

List some more clear messages you might give yourself.

1. _____

2. _____

3. _____

4. _____

5. _____

C. Being a Friend to Others

In math you've learned that 1 + 1 = 2. However, when it comes to friendship, 1 + 1 = 3. Think about it. If you know how to make one good friend, then you can make another. The trick is knowing how to make one good friend. Once you've learned that trick there is no limit to the number of friends you can make. So, 1 + 1 could equal 3 or 10 or 100 or who knows? Read over the next few pages to learn four simple steps you can use to develop friendships. It's called **"The Friendship Model."**

It is important to have an idea of what a friend is like. What qualities or good things do you look for in a friend?

List them below.

1. _____
2. _____
3. _____
4. _____
5. _____

Here are some ideas other students have shared:

Words that Describe a Good Friend

caring	kind	good manners
honest	trustworthy	understanding
shares	giving	accepting
fun to be around	sense of humor	a good listener
flexible	hard working	easy going
doesn't pressure others	stays out of trouble	patient
commonness (shares same interests and hobbies)		

For some students, making friends and keeping friends seems to be easy. However, for many students who are shy, move a lot, or have an attention problem, the process can be frustrating.

The Friendship Model

In "**The Friendship Model**" there are four steps.

1. **Check it Out**
2. **Reach Out**
3. **Try it Out**
4. **Work it Out**

The *first step* is to "**Check Out**" yourself and the kinds of messages you send to others. Are you sending *clear* messages or *muddy* messages to others?

Clear messages are positive messages such as looking at people, smiling, being polite, and helping others. *Muddy* messages are negative messages such as crying, whining, tattling, and pushing.

Make sure you send clear messages to others. You are then more likely to be the type of person others want to be around. Look for friends who also send clear messages back to you.

The *second step* is to "**Reach Out**." This is the step where you need to talk to others. If you don't know what to say, then you can give a *compliment* or you can use an *everyday statement*.

A *compliment* is when you say something nice to someone, such as: "I like your T-shirt," or "You are a good ball player."

An *everyday statement* is a sentence about almost anything, such as: "What is your favorite subject?" "Do you have any brothers or sisters?" "How old are you?" or "What movie is your all-time favorite?"

Can you make up a *compliment*? Write one or two for practice.

1. _____

2. _____

Can you make up an *everyday statement*? Write one or two for practice?

1. _____

2. _____

Conversation Starting

Starting a conversation is a basic skill for developing friendships. Like anything else, it takes practice. Here are some tips for reaching out.

Reach Out

1. *Face the person and make eye contact.*
2. *Greet the other person* by name. Just say hello.
3. *Shake hands* or give the other person "five."
4. *Make small talk.* Discuss whatever you think the other person may be interested in discussing. Topics may include school, sports, the weather, current events, and so forth.

   These are examples of everyday statements.
5. *Give a compliment.* Say something nice to the other person. Compliment the other person's appearance or something the other person does well. Give compliments in an unforced and sincere voice tone.

These are guidelines for starting a conversation. Perhaps the best way to learn these skills is to just watch others around you. Watching certain TV programs offers some good examples of the skill of talking to others. Relax and be yourself. Before long, you'll be meeting lots of interesting people.

The *third step* is to "**Try it Out.**"

When you go to the store to buy a pair of shoes, you try them on before you buy them. Well, the same thing goes with making friends. You should ask yourself whether these students are good for you as friends. Do you feel comfortable being with them? Step three involves deciding who your friends are going to be. Ask yourself about the friend or group, "Is it working?" and "Does it feel okay?"

If the answer is yes, then you move to *step four.* "**Work it Out.**" This means to keep the friendship going. To keep friends you must work hard at being a friend yourself. Good friends usually share, are honest, are good listeners, and care about other people's feelings.

A good friend is not a jealous person. Try hard to be thoughtful and patient. Think before you say something that you might regret.

If your friendships are not working out, then take a **"Time Out"** and ask yourself what is going wrong. Begin by checking yourself out again. Remember to send clear—not muddy—messages. Look for some pals who send clear messages to you.

The following are a couple of reasons why relationships don't work out.

Are You Really Listening?

One of the surest ways to connect with others is to know how to really listen. Listening involves more than hearing others. The following is a list of good listening habits. Place a check (√) by the ones you need to do **more often**.

Do you:

❏ 1. Look directly at the speaker.

❏ 2. Keep eye contact (without staring).

❏ 3. Smile when appropriate.

❏ 4. Slightly lean toward the speaker.

❏ 5. Nod to show you are listening.

❏ 6. Pay attention without interrupting.

❏ 7. Express the feelings of the speaker.
(For example, "I guess you feel **disappointed**.")

❏ 8. Summarize or retell important information that is shared with you. (For example, "You're saying school has been a hassle lately.")

❏ 9. Ask "open questions" about what was said. (Open questions begin with **what, when, how, where** or **who**.)

❏ 10. Make occasional brief verbal responses that show you are listening. (For example, "uh-huh or hmmm.")

Practice Your Listening Skills

To check out your listening skills, get into a group of three. Take turns playing three different roles. Have a conversation leader, a listener, and an observer. While the leader talks about a subject, the listener tries to use the ten listening habits. The observer keeps score of how many of the ten listening habits were used by the assigned listener. The leader can talk about sports, a favorite movie, a hobby, and so forth. Take turns playing each role.

Listening Habits Scoreboard

Put a checkmark by each habit when used appropriately. See if the listener can score a perfect ten.

- ❏ 1. Looks at speaker
- ❏ 2. Keeps eye contact
- ❏ 3. Smiles
- ❏ 4. Leans forward
- ❏ 5. Nods
- ❏ 6. Doesn't interrupt
- ❏ 7. States feelings of speakers
- ❏ 8. Summarizes information
- ❏ 9. Asks open questions
- ❏ 10. Uses brief verbal responses

Push Button Words

The expression "pushing your buttons" means saying or doing something that upsets or angers another person. Words are powerful. It is a good idea to avoid words that lead to conflicts and anger. Sometimes people use certain words in an attempt to be humorous. However, the other person may not think it is so funny and may get angry about what has been said. Other times, certain words are used to hurt others on purpose. Instead of settling a problem, this, of course, makes things worse. People need to recognize words that trigger or "push others' buttons." Push button words are words that are said about another person or group of people. These words involve things that are sensitive to the other person. Everyone has something about which they are sensitive. The following are some examples of subjects about which people don't like to be teased or kidded.

Area of Sensitivity

Talking about someone's...

family	ethnic background
race	religion
age	looks (physical appearance)
weakness	group
job	nationality
handicaps	social status

The rule of thumb is not to talk about others unless you have something good to say. We believe it is a good idea to think about what you are saying and avoid saying anything that may be taken in the wrong way. Play it safe and keep your conversation positive.

Try to remember the four-step friendship model. Think about each step every time you are trying to make and keep your friends. Note the following chart. The chart will help you to remember the four steps. You may want to talk to your school counselor and plan how you may use the four steps.

The Friendship Model

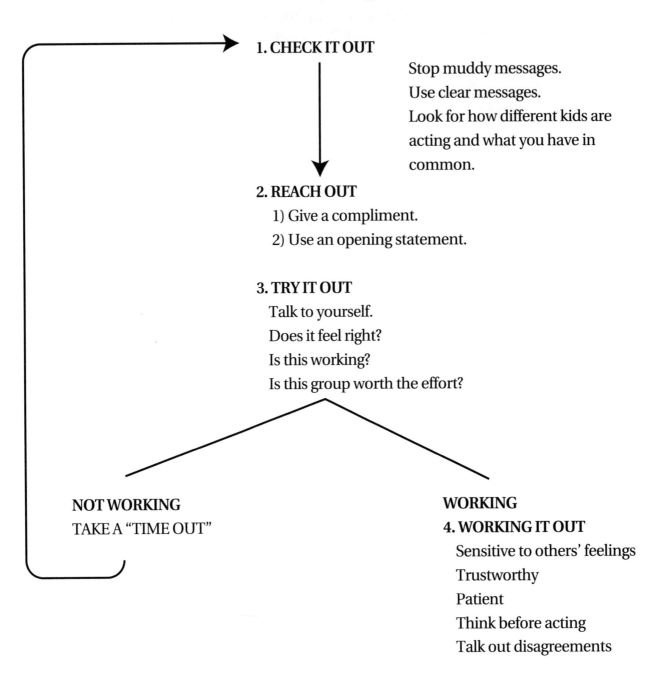

1. CHECK IT OUT

Stop muddy messages.
Use clear messages.
Look for how different kids are acting and what you have in common.

2. REACH OUT

1) Give a compliment.
2) Use an opening statement.

3. TRY IT OUT

Talk to yourself.
Does it feel right?
Is this working?
Is this group worth the effort?

NOT WORKING
TAKE A "TIME OUT"

WORKING
4. WORKING IT OUT
Sensitive to others' feelings
Trustworthy
Patient
Think before acting
Talk out disagreements

Source: Smith, S.J. and Walter, G. (1988). *Four steps to making friends.* Rock Hill, SC: Winthrop University.

D. Assertiveness Skills

It is important to know when to stand alone and when to "fit in." People usually attempt to find the right balance.

Students who have difficulty fitting in with the social expectations of those around them can find themselves in a loneliness trap.

At the same time you don't want others to take advantage of you and make you feel uncomfortable. It is very important to let others know how you feel and what you need. However, this must be done in an appropriate, assertive way. Being assertive means to tell others how you feel by demonstrating confidence and not hurting others.

I Messages

Part of being assertive is being able to tell others how you feel and what you think. This needs to be done in a way that does not provoke or start a fight. Instead, you can express yourself in a way that lets others know you have a concern about what is happening. One great way to do this is to use "I messages." "I messages" use the following simple four steps:

1.	Say the person's name	"Carla,"
2.	Tell how you feel	"I feel angry..."
3.	Tell why	"When you come into my room without knocking."
4.	Tell what you want	"Please knock first."

When a person speaks up in a firm but polite way, often times the situation improves. The trick is getting in the habit of using "I messages." With practice, you can use them very effectively.

Caution: Do not overuse "I messages." They are best used when someone is doing something too often which bothers you, or in cases when someone has done one thing in particular which you **really** don't like. Use "I messages" just when really needed. Then they are taken more seriously.

Another caution: In cases of bullying or physical violence, "I messages" will likely *not* work. In this case, get an adult to handle the problem.

Practice

Make up some "I messages" for the following situations. Write out your "I message" by using the four steps.

Situation 1

Someone has been constantly trying to copy your homework.

I Message_____, _____
                  (Name)   (Feeling)

_____   _____
        (Why)   (What you want)

Situation 2

A group of kids is trying to get you to take drugs.

I Message_____, _____
                  (Name)   (Feeling)

_____   _____
        (Why)   (What you want)

Situation 3

Your best friend is always late. You have to wait and wait before this person arrives.

I Message_____, _____
                  (Name)   (Feeling)

_____   _____
        (Why)   (What you want)

A Kid's Guide to Forming Good Relationships and "Fitting In"

Self-Control

Part of being assertive is using self-control. People feel like hitting or yelling at others when a conflict arises. This is when a person needs to stay under control or trouble is sure to follow. The following ideas can help to overcome anger and hopefully work out the problem in a good way.

1. Stop and give yourself permission to think. Think about the best thing to do in this situation.

2. Try to relax. Take a deep breath.

3. Use an "I message." State why you are angry.

4. Try to settle the problem or walk away if the matter is getting worse.

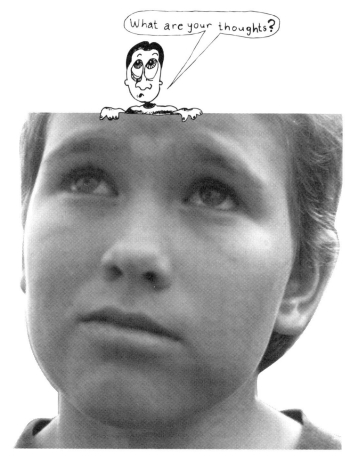

Katherine Gillen

Getting With It

Who Has The Control?

Listed below are 15 words or phrases concerning getting along with people. Some of the words represent behaviors of which you have control. Write those numbers *inside* the body outline. For the behavior words of which you do not have control, write those numbers *outside* the body outline.

1. attending school regularly
2. crime in the neighborhood
3. who your friends are
4. good personal hygiene
5. student attitudes
6. being punctual
7. following the school dress code
8. the school you attend
9. good eye contact
10. grades
11. a friendly smile
12. hurtful behaviors by others
13. family divorce
14. giving compliments
15. a friend shoplifting

Maggie McCaskill

Remember the one person who you can control is yourself. It is impossible to change others, but you can always strive to be the best you can be. Keep working on yourself and you will find that good friendships will follow.

Standing up for Yourself

Another thing to consider is to memorize an assertive statement such as the one below. Use it when someone is trying to put you down or make you do something that is not in your best interest.

You may want to memorize a statement like the following and use it as needed.

> *"When you keep pressuring me to do something I don't want to do, it makes me think you don't care about me."*

Knowing how to say no is another issue when confronted with peer pressure. Try to put into practice the following ideas. You can get very good at taking care of yourself and not getting talked into things that are not in your best interest.

Assertive Responses

1. Look the person right in the eyes.
2. Speak up.
3. Say no right away and walk away.
4. Don't explain or apologize.
5. Mean what you say and say what you mean.

E. Identifying Your Support System

In your school, there is likely a support group for you to talk about how to better "fit in." Ask your counselor or a teacher for information about small group counseling. Support groups can help you to see that you are not the only one dealing with this concern. Many kids your age meet to encourage each other and to discuss ideas for improving relationships. The group offers a safe place for you to discuss your feelings and to enjoy being with others.

Helpful People

Just as important as an ongoing support group are individuals with whom you feel comfortable discussing your situation. Your school counselor and other trusted adults can be counted on to be helpful. It is a good idea to build a network of caring people, both adults and children. Trusted adults may include a parent, coach, teacher, counselor, best friend's mother, religious leader, and so forth.

Friendships with peers may grow out of a support group and other activities in which you may participate. Clubs and after school activities are a good way to develop friendships and to focus on good things that will help you to move along with life.

What does your support team look like? On the following page, fill in as many circles as possible. Be sure to include individuals and groups who are helpful to you. Remember, you don't have to be the "Lone Ranger." There are many people who care. You can develop your support team as large as you would like. It seems to gradually grow as you reach out.

Individuals and Groups
That Make Up My Support Team

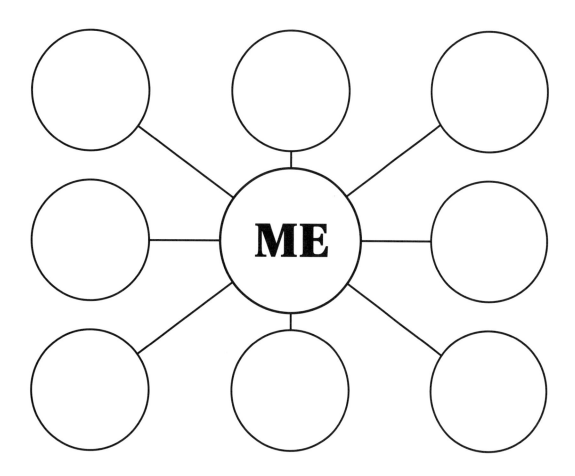

Throughout this book you have been reading and thinking about ways to better "fit in" with those who you care about. The people in your support system can help you present the "best" you. If at times you feel overwhelmed with the idea of trying to change too many behaviors at one time, then you must decide which skills you need to change the most.

It is always helpful to get ideas or feedback from people in your support system as to which behaviors they believe you really need to change.

Do the following steps to decide where to start.

1. Discuss the behaviors from the "Checklist on Nonverbal Communication" on pages 42 and 43 that you listed as needing improvement.

2. Write these areas down and then discuss which ones need the most improvement.

3. List your top three in order, with #1 being the most important.

   1. _____

   2. _____

   3. _____

4. Talk to your support team about activities or projects which will help you to improve these behaviors.

Good communication, both verbally and nonverbally, is the key to unlocking happy or satisfying relationships. In order to "fit in" and feel good about yourself, it is important to evaluate yourself often. By reading and practicing the skills in this book, you will feel as if you are "Getting With It."

Good Luck!

References

Frank, K.E., & Smith, S.J. (1994). *Getting a grip on ADD: A kid's guide to understanding and coping with attention disorders.* Minneapolis, MN: Educational Media Corporation.

Frank, K.E., & Smith-Rex, S.J. (1995). *Getting a life of your own: A kid's guide to understanding and coping with family alcoholism.* Minneapolis, MN: Educational Media Corporation.

Frank, K.E., & Smith-Rex, S.J. (1996). *Getting over the blues: A kid's guide to understanding and coping with depression.* Minneapolis, MN: Educational Media Corporation.

Smith, S.J., & Walter, G. (1988). *Four steps to making friends.* Rock Hill, SC: Winthrop University.